Journey of the Heart
Season by Season

Journey of the Heart
Season by Season
© 2013 Mid Stutsman

Cover photo; Book Layout; Interior Design and Photography; Author Photo: by *Images Inspired*

© Mid L. Stutsman www.midspoint.com

May you always be in wonder of the Seasons with the changes and beauty each one brings. Created by God, they are an offering of Grace and a promise He will see us through to the end.

Mid

I ran with the wind today,
and my heart felt the depth of
being.
I held a whisper in my hands
and listened until it blew away.
I am wiser now.

Summer

*Come run with me in the cool
mist of the morning to where the
red dawn rises . . .
to where a glint of gold splits
the heavens open,
and there, together, we will
splash through the endless
waves of summer's promise.*

Raindrops sparkle in the sunlight . . . crystals dancing on the ends of flower petals and leaves, as reality morphs into a fantasy world!

When Warm Breezes Blow

Honeysuckle days, and the romantic spell of
heirloom roses warmed by the Sun,
when it reaches its fingertips
through the lengthening hours, caressing winter skin
to a darkened amber glaze.

Barefoot excursions wind through my mind
down secluded beaches, leaving footprints at the
edge of the ocean's ebb and flow,
while starry nights float through the ageless wonder
of a lover's splendor.

Memories hover with hummingbird passion,
on a quest for life's defining nectar, and flutter past
on butterfly wings, until,
wrapped in the echo of my sighs, I feel the wind
beckon . . . "Dream no longer."

The blossoms have opened, the morning is sweetly perfumed, and the hummingbirds have honeysuckle breath . . .

SUMMER'S DAZE

Summer flopped down on the soft green grass and rested her chin in her hands. Succumbing to her deep sigh, the tree leaves fluttered high above her. Soon, her stay would come to a close. Anxious, she surveyed her handiwork.

Flowers now put all their energy into their last blossoms. Vegetables crowded each other, vying for more space in the gardens. Even the air was perfumed with fruity smells, but the daylight grew shorter and drained her energy. She still had the goldenrod and bittersweet to coax into bloom, the grapes to ripen and the fields . . . oh the fields!

As she swept the damp curls back from her forehead, a sudden breeze blew cool across her face. She closed her eyes. A smile teased the corners of her red lips. "Is that you, Autumn?"

Autumn, lovely in a russet dappled dress and scarlet slippers, appeared at Summer's side and sat down. She placed her hands behind her and leaned her head back, letting her long auburn hair tickle the blades of grass. "I'm never able to sneak up on you am I, Summer?" She tried pouting, though rather unconvincingly.

Summer didn't answer, but she did giggle, which prompted Autumn to sit up and clasp her hands around her knees. She cast an admiring glance her way. "You've completely outdone yourself this time, my Sunny Friend. The Creator is very pleased!"

A look of uncertainty clouded Summer's eyes as she turned over on her stomach. "Oh Autumn, do you really think so?"

"Mmm hmm, I do." Autumn nodded her head, her smile sweet and genuine. "Just look at the verdant fields, the roadsides and gardens splashed with bright bold flowers, the trees magnificently lush with mature foliage."

"But you know I'm not quite done," Summer worried. Her voice trailed off as she envisioned what she had left to do.

"I know." Autumn bent down and cupped a red clover blossom in her hands, inhaling the deliciously sweet fragrance. As she let go, the blossom shivered and brown fingerprints appeared on its dainty pink face. "Oops! Guess I'm a little early."

She reached over and lifted a wayward curl off of Summer's glistening neck and wound it around the rose tucked into her wispy blonde tresses. This time she was careful not to touch the flower. "It's just that you look so exhausted, and I am anxious to get busy this fall. But perhaps I should leave and let you finish."

At this remark Summer rolled onto her back again. She held her arm over her face to shield it from the late afternoon sun and contemplated her companion. Come to think of it, she was tired and hot, and a little break just might do her a world of good.

"Maybe," Summer hesitated for a moment and then blurted out, "maybe . . . I mean, could you just take over for a week or so? Until I can get my strength back? I only have a few more projects to accomplish."

Her bare toes twitched as she envisioned dangling them in a cold, swift-running stream 'neath the pale moonlight. She waited for Autumn's response.

Autumn glanced sideways at her and laid her head on her knees.

Summer grew nervous. Surely her good nature would compel Autumn to consider her offer, but even if it was only out of a sense of compassion, she desperately needed her friend's help.

"You really do look worn to a frazzle," Autumn mused. "So, you just want me to stay for a week, right?"

"Yes," Summer answered, hope surging through her. "But remember, mainly at night and only to bring the temperature down a bit."

"Yes, yes, I know. But don't you forget that you're supposed be resting. Oh, and, um, Summer?" Autumn's voice cooled to a whisper, "You might want to change your dress."

Summer looked down and surveyed her soft shimmering gown, spun from the morning dew and trimmed with golden rays. It was all rumpled and frayed. The flowers woven into it now hung limp, their once vibrant colors beginning to fade.

Embarrassed, she ran her hands across her garment and tried to smooth out the wrinkles. "Of course I'm going to change. It's just, well, it's been weeks since I've had a break, and with no rain lately for a shower . . ."

Autumn reached over and patted her arm. "It's okay, I understand. And don't worry, I can take care of a shower for you."

With that, she sprang to her feet and offered Summer a hand. "Now, git, and don't forget to return the favor. You have to come visit me during the fall!"

Summer's bronzed face turned radiant with relief as she let Autumn help her up. She drew her friend into a warm embrace. "Somehow, I knew you'd come through!"

As the two seasons stood with hands clasped, the hot sultry day turned pleasant and mild. Then Autumn let go and twirled in the breeze swirling around them. Her dress rustled softly, echoing her delight.

"What do you think," she teased, the sunbeams sparkling in her coppery green eyes, "should I change into something a little more . . . summery?"

Flitting among vibrant petals,
graceful blurs sip on nectar . . .

Life should be so lovely!

Farewell to Summer

I dance through the fire forged upon Fall's anvil,
and shiver with anxiety through Winter's icy breath,
waiting with longing
until Spring coaxes me into her pastel sunshine.
But only Summer has a hold on my spirit,
drenching me
in her delicious warmth.
I roam long stretches of sandy beaches and watch
cerulean waves merge with the sky.
Mountainous clouds, just out of reach, remind me
of a coming day
when they will glide between my outstretched
hands.
Riots of color and scents, beyond a perfumer's
touch, wrap around my senses.
Winged creatures of grace and beauty teach me to
hope.
Ah, Summer, sweet Summer. I beg her to stay, but
she slips between my grasp.
Yet, like a best friend who must move away, she
always promises to come back and visit
. . . next year

Autumn

If only love could be won by deeds, then would fall have my heart and return my affections

Autumn's Secret

Streams of leafy golden rays
filter through my world surreal,
now awash with scarlet haze
as russet patterned days reveal
a festivity,
awakening me
from the lull of summer's
somnolent green to a greater
celebration now concealed:
a secret kept amid the blaze
until the Harvest of the Age.

Tapestry

Autumn appears at God's command ~
her leafy locks pinned up with an array of
jewels
that sparkle beneath her sapphire eyes,
and with cool whispered sighs,
she weaves the finest tapestry . . .
unequaled in color,
unmatched in beauty,
and drapes it like a shawl over the
land.

Fall's Fleeting Fancy

Morning sun touches the
sad leaves of summer's end,
until Fall rushes in
with nails painted ruby red.
Trees display her jeweled
fingerprints, and drab fades
away to sparkles dancing,
before she kisses them goodbye
and shushes them to forever sleep.

An Ode to Autumn

She moves like a whisper on the breeze,
silently she walks the land,
setting fire to the slumbering trees,
who shiver 'neath her icy hand.
There's warmth in her eyes,
but her breath is cool,
and fair though the skies,
Autumn's no fool,
for her heart tells her Winter is not far away,
so swiftly she sets the whole landscape ablaze!
Then she disappears
with tears in her eyes,
for she cannot bear to see her leaves die.
And as silently as she came one day,
Autumn walks back
into the chilling haze.

Jack Frost's Diamonds

Jack sat with his back against the trunk of a massive maple tree and drew his fingers across one of the fallen leaves. At his touch, an intricate pattern appeared, and the edges of the leaves sparkled. His artistic skills had no rival as he followed Autumn's trek throughout the land. He drew beautiful crystal images on her handiwork and left frosty swirls on many a window pane. He transformed dreary days into breathless creations, which elicited the admiration of all who came upon them. All that is, except for one lovely creature . . . Summer.

When he sighed, his breath settled over a ragged weed, just as the sun peeked out and revealed the new diamond-encrusted garment.

Upon seeing its smile of gratitude, Jack jumped to his feet and spread out his hands, bestowing his icy blessings on the surrounding landscape.

If only the love of his life could appreciate his gift. But Summer spurned his advances and guarded the works of her hands with warm care. Any attempt on his part to show her the depth of his love was quickly dismissed by a wave of her hands, and it slowly melted away.

Only Autumn accepted his company, and only Autumn understood his plight. She joined him one day and listened as he vented his despair and frustration. "I have nothing to give her that she will accept as a token of my love. She doesn't want anything to do with me."

"Jack, I don't think it has anything to do with you personally."

"What do you mean?"

Autumn bit down on her lower lip before she answered. "Well, it's how you approach her. She is very jealous of her accomplishments, and your touch ruins all she's worked so hard to bring forth during her stay. I've never told you this, because I didn't want to hurt your feelings, but she asks me to visit once in a while toward the end of her stays . . . just to cool things down a bit."

Jack looked at her, his eyes wide with unbelief. "You get to visit Summer? All this time, and you've never said anything?"

"I told you, I didn't want to . . ."

"Yeah, I heard you. But my feeling *are* hurt."

"Please don't be mad. I love your gift of making things so beautiful. The diamonds and sparkles light up my stay. Wait, that's it!"

Jack cast a wary glance her way. "What is *it*?"

"Diamonds! What girl doesn't love diamonds? You could find her when she's away and relaxing during my next visit and give her diamonds. She only leaves when she's tired and hot. If you handed her some of your gorgeous ice crystals and told her you just wanted her to be cool and comfortable, well, maybe she'd see you in a different light!"

"I don't know. You really think she'd let me get near enough to explain?"

"I do, especially if you find her right at the beginning when she's desperate for a refreshing change. It's worth a try . . . if you truly have feelings for her."

Jack's knees went weak at the thought of another scorching rejection by Summer, but Autumn was right. He had to show his love somehow. This just might work.

As it turned out, Autumn proved to be the best of friends. At the appointed time, Jack not only knew when Summer would leave, but he found out her exact location as well. All he had to do was summon the courage to be there at the right moment.

When he did, he came upon the lovely creature deep in a forest, where a tiny stream gurgled past her feet. She sat on the edge of a fallen log with her head in her hands and wept because the water had become warm. The cool respite from the heat she had longed for was not to be. Thinking fast, but staying out of sight, Jack dipped his hands into the stream and waited.

A quiet hush rushed past him, and he knew this was his one big chance. "Summer?" He breathed out her name and let it float by her on a gentle breeze.

"Who's there?"

Jack stepped out from the shadows.

Summer sat up straight, her eyes misty with emotion. "Jack? You, you did that for me?"

Jack nodded cautiously, and brought his hands out from behind his back. Small crystals of ice sparkled like diamonds in Summer's presence, and she caught her breath at the sight of them.

"I made these for you." He moved slowly toward her, and to his surprise, she held out her hands. As the crystals spilled into her warm embrace and slipped through her fingers, he continued to form them until she closed her eyes and smiled.

It was all he had hoped for, and it was then that their hands touched . . . ever so softly. Cold melted. Warmth chilled. And the world around them sighed.

That night, as the evening breeze ventured through the forest, the moon looked down on two unlikely lovers, walking hand in hand. A diamond sparkled on Summer's finger, a forever promise from Jack that he would be there any time she needed him.

They both understood the crystal wouldn't last come morning light. It didn't need to, it was a promise he intended to keep, and a gift she would anticipate each season.

After all, as Autumn so well knew . . . what girl doesn't love diamonds?

Winter

Sunbeams set freshly fallen snow
afire with diamond dust sparkles,
as fantasy aspires to set
imaginings aglow, in winter
hearts too soon grown cold.

Wintry Thoughts

Snow is falling,
calling to that inner joy
of winter frolic and white
lace covering,
hovering with icy memories
of angelic lines,
defined by the innocence
we rolled into piles
of forever snowmen . . .
with forever smiles.

That Sly Old Man

Snowflakes, crystal patterns, icicles . . .
those wintry prisms trapping whatever light
is available and transforming the drab
and dreary into a fantasy other-world
of twinkling, shimmering, sparkling
wonders. There is a mesmerizing quality
to the frozen atmosphere. One might see it as an
apologetic gift given in return for stripping the
surroundings of their life and color at the end of the
year . . . a solace, if you will, for the shivering,
freezing misery bestowed upon
us by the harsh North Wind. I'll never have
a love affair with Old Man Winter, but if truth be
told, I secretly admire his dazzling attempts to win
my heart.

Snowfall

Winter's breath, icy cold
blowing down through dreams of old,
falling softly through the night,
casting lacy shadows bold
upon a bed of downy white.

OLD MAN WINTER

A blustery gust picked up loose bits of snow and ice and sent them scudding across the frozen northern plains. They were on an important mission now, for the North Wind had just ordered them to find the Old Man and wake him from his deep, wintry sleep.

The sky above turned gray as they howled out his name through the wind, but they didn't have to call long, for off in the distance they saw a huge white mound tremble. As the snow started breaking up, big chunks tumbled down and an icy figure emerged.

Stretching and shaking off crusty bits of frost, Winter's piercing blue eyes caught a glimpse of the sun parting the clouds to watch the annual event.

"I'm awake, I'm awake . . ." The Old Man yawned, dismissing the sun with a wave, and the clouds moved together again as if he had just drawn a privacy curtain. "I have a long hard season ahead," he made excuse. "Besides," he continued, mumbling to himself, "I need some time to check on Autumn's progress without the likes of you peering over my shoulders."

"Autumn . . ." He sighed. Her very name conjured up images that led him into a thoughtful mode. This year he had to plan his arrival better so as not to pop in when summer was visiting her.

"She's a sensitive season that one, and beautiful too," he reminisced. Cool in nature herself, Autumn appeared to enjoy his company and was always grateful when he laid a pure white blanket of snow over her dying leaves. Sadly, it seemed destined to be that they would have to part company not too long after he arrived each year.

"If only she wouldn't cry when she's summoned south this time," the Old Man lamented.

He was never really sure if her tears rained down because of their parting, or if they were for her beloved leaves. He only knew that each time it happened it stirred within him rare feelings of compassion and tenderness. It would even take him a few weeks to recover before he could feel cold-hearted enough to produce a good blizzard or snow squall! Then the rest of his lonely stay would be spent in keeping up with the many demands of the season.

Meanwhile, curious as to the delay, the sun spotted a thin layer in the clouds and broke through again just in time to catch Winter beginning to melt into his warm thoughts of Autumn.

     "Winter, if I didn't know better, I'd say you almost looked happy," the sun whispered down through the Arctic wind.

     The taunting breeze disrupted the Old Man's reverie and he quickly regained his composure. Glancing around to make sure no one else saw him getting mushy, he scowled at the sun.

     "What do you know?" he snarled, hoping to regain his notorious image. "Besides, you're too close for comfort and it's slowing me down and, and . . ." his voice rose to a fevered pitch as he roared, "now I'm going to be late!"

Averting the intruder's insolent glare, he whipped his heavy cloak around him and shook his fist. "Don't you have somewhere else to go?"

Wearing a smug grin, the sun wisely ignored the Old Man's fierce growls and silently sank beneath the vermilion horizon, taking his secret with him.

Still embarrassed, Winter kicked up the melted snow around him in a tantrum, and froze it with an icy blast. A stormy look overtook his eyes as he summoned the North Wind, who blew in at his command. With the frigid air swirling around him, he trudged off, sputtering and muttering something about being too old for this. Behind him, the freezing rain left a crunchy trail so he could find his way back before Spring.

Snowstorm

The West wind
unleashed all its fury
in a flurry of downy might.
Snowflakes flying in a blinding haze,
and I'm amazed
at the beauty of white.

A veil of white drapes the land with elegant beauty. All is still, but I hear the trill of Spring, calling beneath a drift of snow.

Spring

Early morning woods blanketed with flowers and mossy green dreams. It's quiet with only bird song and the crunch of last winter's remains.

Dancing with Spring

Come, Spring, sprout you wings
and hasten to my garden.
Feather your nest with warm sunbeams
and lichen from the mossy streams,
then bid farewell to wintry dreams
and dance with me in the mornin'.

SPRING'S LAMENT

Fresh and beautiful in her new gown of green, Spring picked a fragrant wood violet and tucked it into her long flowing hair. With a gleam in her eyes, she playfully tiptoed up behind Winter and reached around to lay a gentle hand upon his cheek.

Now with anyone else, her warm touch would have been met with eager anticipation, but when Winter sensed her presence he turned, and with crystal blue eyes scowling, he coldly brushed her aside. As Spring's hands rushed to cover her face, the Old Man's frosty eyebrows relaxed, but he quickly shook off any feelings of regret and brusquely walked away.

"Winter, wait," Spring called out, but her pleas returned to her unanswered, leaving her forlorn and shivering in the wake of his icy rejection. As she watched his snowy figure disappear into the mist, her tears rained down, splashing mud on the flowers awakening beneath her feet.

Since the beginning of seasons, Spring has followed after Winter, trying to win over his frozen heart. But each year it seems her endeavors at acquiring his attention only serve to provoke him all the more. As soon as he sees her approaching, with the sun at her beck and call, he'll display the cantankerous nature of an old recluse whose solitude has been irreverently disrupted.

Oh, that she is lovely, he can't deny, but her emotionally windy and capricious ways he finds absolutely intolerable. Why, just the thought of all her happy little colors and enticing scents are enough to send him off on a stormy rampage across the land. In a blinding fury of snow and bitter cold, he'll vent his anger out on anyone or anything who dares to respond to her warm seductions.

Then there are times when he will simply turn his back on her, and just to be spiteful, disappear into the earth without even saying good-bye. There, he'll leave her to weep uncontrollably in Summer's arms.

Ah, but ever the hopeful romantic, Spring will appear again the next year, flashing her flirtatious smile. And Winter will look over his shoulders to find her displaying her flowery charms in an attempt to gain his affections and change his cold-hearted nature.

Of course, he will throw a snowy fit or two and maybe even toy with her feelings once in awhile, though never letting her come too close, for he knows full well that succumbing to her warmth will inevitably prove to be his demise.

Something she just doesn't seem to understand. But then, hasn't it ever been thus?

*I stroll through forests of green
leaves, budding
beneath a cloudless sky . . .
sunlight filters through the
branches, echoing their tranquil
sighs.*

A silent song of praise plays through the seasons. Thankfulness harmonizes with the love I long to express as I experience each one.

God knows~He hears~He accepts